FOUL FACTS: SCHOOL

The Worst Days of Your Life

The following Watts Paperbacks are also available:

FOUL FACTS

Skin & Bone
Gruesome Grub
Flops and Failures

WHIZZKIDS

101 Things to Do With Your Body
101 Ways to Test Your Friends
101 Things to Do
101 Things to Know

BRAIN BUSTERS

Word Whackers
Travel Teasers
Cryptic Codes
Animal Word Whackers

FOUL FACTS: SCHOOL
The Worst Days of Your Life

Steve Skidmore
Steve Barlow
Illustrated by Alan Rowe

WATTS BOOKS

Watts Books
96 Leonard Street
London EC2 4RH

Franklin Watts
14 Mars Road
Lane Cove
NSW 2066

UK ISBN 0 7496 1641 5
Dewey Decimal Classification 371

10 9 8 7 6 5 4 3 2 1

Illustrations by
Alan Rowe

A CIP catalogue record for this book is available from the British Library.

Printed in Great Britain by
The Guernsey Press Company Ltd., Guernsey, Channel Islands.
Designed and Typeset by Harrington Consultancy Ltd
Karen House 1/11 Baches Street London N1 6DL

CONTENTS

INTRODUCTION

This book gives you ALL THE KNOWN FACTS* about schools:

What they are
Where they began
Why they developed
How to survive them.

It explains how the half-human Blog the Caveman has evolved into Fred Bloggs, Superpupil, the fully-trained end-product of the modern education system.

But before we begin our journey, what IS a school? Where, in fact, does the word "school" come from? We're glad you asked us that…

WICKED WORDS

School It comes from the Greek "schole", meaning "leisure" – which shows that the Greeks had a pretty sick sense of humour! Similarly, the Roman word for school, "ludus", means "play". One Roman scholar suggested that the name was chosen because it was the opposite of what really went on in schools and was less likely to put the pupils off attending.

(That is, all the facts known to the authors.)*

Education The verb "educate" comes from a Latin word, "educare", meaning to bring up (children, not lunch).

Gymnasium This was a name that the ancient Greeks gave to their schools. They did much more there than run around before being forced to have a cold shower.

Grammar In Roman schools, a teacher of reading and writing was called a "grammatistes", because he worked with the letters of the alphabet ("grammata"). The Romans called language schools grammar schools, a term still used in parts of Britain.

Syllabus Roman books were long strips of papyrus on wooden rollers, so it was difficult to find the bit you wanted. Each roll came with a ticket, called a "syllabus", showing its contents. We now use this word to mean a programme of study.

"Young People Today"

In their exhaustive historical research, the authors have discovered that some things haven't changed at all. For instance, here are some complaints about behaviour in schools hundreds of years ago:

Young people today wear their hair too long and have too much jewellery. They should crop their hair close and

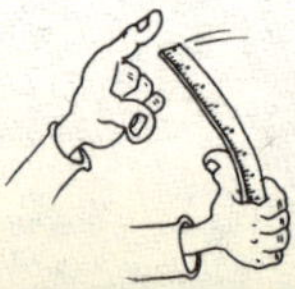

leave it unadorned.
What's more, they are lazy...
...they spend too much time putting their hair in waves...
...and they dance and sing too loudly.

When students are bored, they: ...nod, though they haven't a clue what the lesson is about...ask silly questions to show off...grin or laugh at the serious bits...look all round the room...twist in their seats...whisper, and yawn.

These complaints were noted by the Greek philosopher Diogenes in the fifth century BC, and by the ancient Roman historians Seneca and Plutarch. So, the next time your teacher goes on about your not paying attention in class, show him or her this page and blame the whole thing on genetics!

BUT, you may be saying to yourselves, I KNOW what schools ARE. After all, I go to one, worse luck. I haven't forked out my money to find out things I already know; how did it all **start**? Read on, and all will be revealed...

FROM CAVE TO CLASSROOM

We don't know much about how the first people learned things because they were pre-historic, which means that they lived before history had been invented – lucky old them! We can guess, by looking at societies that have existed since ancient times, such as the Australian Aborigines or the Silent People of the Kalahari Desert.

Blog the Caveman, 5,000 years BS (Before Schools)

Your great-great-great-great-and-a-few-hundred-times-more-great-grandfather wouldn't have gone to school, but he would still have learnt things. We can guess that he would have had lessons in Natural History…to teach him to hunt, because in those days you had to kill your own dinner, provided that your dinner didn't kill you first.

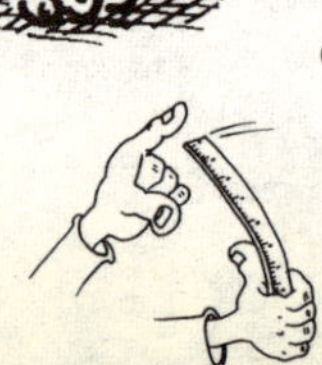

Blog would have been too busy to sit around in a classroom. He would have had to help his family find food and build shelters, and later on look after sheep and goats and grow crops. Blog's family would have been bigger than the sort many of us are used to. Aunts, uncles, cousins, grandparents and so on all lived in the same group, so Blog would have had plenty of other kids to play with.

Blog's family would have told stories about everything: the things that happened to them, how the world was created, and why things are as they are. These stories were not written down. The older people would make them up or remember them; and when Blog had heard them often enough, he would be able to remember them too. Of course, now we have books, cassettes, TV and videos, we can't remember anything more complicated than "Knock Knock" jokes. This is called Progress.

School

We know that Blog learned art, because many of the pictures he and his friends painted are still around.

However, it must be said that Blog would compare very badly with the sophisticated youth of today.

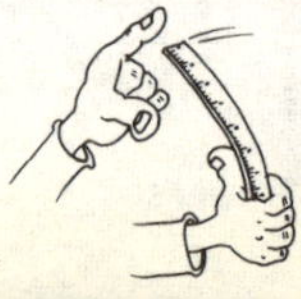

FOUL FIRST SCHOOL FACTS

Before schools began, people just learned what they needed to survive, any old how and from anyone who happened to be around. This happy state of affairs went on until some clever Greeks decided that having one person teach a group THE SAME THINGS AT THE SAME TIME would be more efficient. They invented **The School**, and the world has been a less happy place ever since!

The Greeks Have A Word For It

However, since the word is rude and we're not allowed to print it, we'll pass straight on to:

A Day in the Life of Fredos Blogidopoulos, Athens, 1000 BC

I met my instructor at the gate of the Gymnasium as Apollo's Chariot carried the burning orb of the sun over the horizon, its light bursting forth like a magnificent shield of shining gold.
My instructor, marvelling at the sight, said unto me, "What time do you call this, then?"

First hour - reading in the library. Our library is the greatest of any Gymnasium in all Greece, I do believe, for we have almost twenty books.

In the Second hour we were called upon to recite. My recitation was an epic poem on the subject of "The Good Ship Aphrodite."

In the Third hour I was whipped for reciting rude verses. Such behaviour is frowned upon in the Gymnasium.

The Fourth hour was given over to writing. I had to write out fifty times, "I must not rhyme "Aphrodite" with

"Lady's Nightie".

In the Fifth hour, we sang. My instructor went for a lie down, saying he had a headache.

In the Sixth hour, I played the Lyre. My instructor came and listened to me. When I went home, my mother asked me why I was wearing my Lyre as a necklace.

SCHOOLS TODAY: FOUL FACTS AND FIGURES

When the poor old Greeks invented schools, they can hardly have known what they were letting all the rest of us in for, or they'd probably never have started the beastly things! Just look how things have turned out!

Watch out, there's a teacher about!

There are 45 million teachers in the world. This means that one out of every 100 people in the world is a teacher! YUK! There are over half a million teachers in the UK! UK! We mean, YUK!

How much do you cost?*

Fancy going to the most expensive Public School in the UK? Sorry, this is for boys only, not girls. If you do, then go to Harrow School in Middlesex. Parents pay nearly £12,500 a year for their sons to board at this school.

If you don't want to be a boarder, the most expensive school for day pupils is Charterhouse in Essex. It costs only about £10,000 a year. And girls are allowed in the sixth form! Hooray!

The UK government spends about £2,000 a year for every pupil attending a state school.

** 1994 figures*

School

The Oldest in Britain

There is a big argument over which is the oldest school in Britain. Two schools claim the title. King's School in Canterbury was founded sometime between AD 597 and AD 604, by St Augustine. Cor Tewdws (College of Theodosius) in South Glamorgan claims that it was already going strong in AD 446, but was burnt down (HOORAY!) and had to be rebuilt (BOO!) in AD 508.

The largest school in the world

In 1988-89, Rizal High School in Manila in the Philippines had 16,458 students.

UK schools with the most pupils

In Britain in 1990-91, Exmouth Community College had 2,036 students. This isn't the greatest number ever known. In 1975, Banbury Comprehensive had 2,767. Lucky them!

The pupil attending the most schools

How many different schools have you been to? Three, four, ten? We bet you can't beat Wilma Williams from the USA! She went to 265 schools between 1933 and 1943. Her parents were in show business and moved around a lot!

How much do teachers earn?

Ask all your teachers and see how many say MIND YOUR OWN BUSINESS! and how many say NOT ENOUGH!
We bet these are the only answers you'll get!

PUBLIC AND PRIVATE

The names "Public School" and "Private School" are confusing. Let's say a group of lawyers decided to start a school. If they wanted the school to teach their own children, not anybody else's, it would be a Private School for Lawyers. By contrast, Public Schools would let in pupils from any families who could pay enough. That's how it was in medieval times.

Nowadays, Private Schools are public, as they will usually let in anybody who pays enough. People also pay to go to Public Schools, except in Scotland, where going to a public school is free.

We hope that clears that up!

How many hours will you spend at school?

Days spent at school every year: 190*.
Hours spent at school every year: 1,140.
If you stay on until you are 18, you are at school for 15,960 hours.

AND REMEMBER THIS DOESN'T INCLUDE HOMEWORK TIME!

IT'S A LOT OF HOURS! Linford Christie can run 100 metres in 10 seconds. In 15,960 hours he could run 574,560 kilometres, which means he could run round the world 14 times.**

** Some lucky people will have less, some unfortunates will have more.*
*** You may not find this very interesting, but it took us a long time to work it out, so don't START, OK?*

EVER BEEN BORED IN LESSONS?

Create your own Foul Facts form to discover how many hours a year you waste with BORING lessons.

STAGE 1

NUMBER OF LESSONS IN A DAY ☐

Multiply by 5 to get

NUMBER OF LESSONS PER WEEK ☐

STAGE 2

HOW MANY OF THESE LESSONS
DO YOU FIND BORING? ☐

Multiply by 39 (average number of weeks you spend at school) to get

NUMBER OF BORING LESSONS PER YEAR ☐

STAGE 3

HOW LONG IS A LESSON? (in minutes) ☐

Multiply by your number of boring lessons per year to get

NUMBER OF MINUTES BORED PER YEAR ☐

Divide by 60 to get

NUMBER OF HOURS BORED AT SCHOOL PER YEAR ☐

STAGE 4

List the things you would rather be doing than being bored at school.

....

....

....

Present this to your parent/teacher or anyone else you wish to complain to.

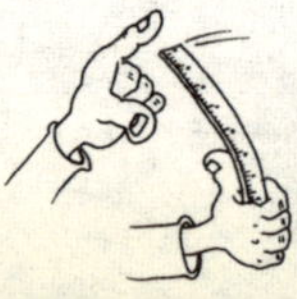

EDUCATION IN ANCIENT ROME

Ancient Greek schools were what we would call secondary schools and colleges. The Romans, being a hard-hearted lot, decided that there was no reason why little kids shouldn't suffer as well.

Many things that we see as normal parts of schooling started off in Roman times.

Teachers were usually slaves. ("So what else is new?" your teacher will say). This was because Roman citizens were usually too busy doing other things, such as watching gladiators hack bits off each other at the circus, conquering other nations, poisoning their friends and generally being civilized. Roman parents admired the Ancient Greeks and wanted their children to learn to

speak, read and write Greek, as well as their own language, Latin. They would snap up almost anybody who spoke Greek as a tutor. The man who taught the young Emperor Caligula was a Greek-speaking mule-driver, which may help to explain why his pupil turned out to be totally *nutso*...

Bringing up Baby...

A Roman nurse ("educatrix") often chewed Baby's food into small morsels before popping it into Baby's mouth. It meant that anyone wanting to poison the child only poisoned the nurse first!

ROMAN SCHOOLS

The Aristocracy

Rich Romans bought or hired "pedagogues" to teach their children in their own homes. Many of them were prisoners of war, but some were exiles down on their luck. Crates of Mallos was a Greek ambassador who got stuck in Rome when he broke his leg falling into a sewer. He couldn't travel, so he gave lectures instead.

Many noble families hired a whole staff of foreign tutors for their children. Often the pedagogue was a stern teacher and served as guardian, able to dish out beatings if he wished. Older children had tutors called praeceptors, who dealt with more advanced knowledge.

Slaves

Slaves also received education in the houses of their masters. Sometimes they took their lessons alongside the master's children. Some masters sent their slaves to join the lessons given in other households, by teachers they considered the best. They did not do this out of kindness to the slaves. They knew that slaves who could read and write could be sold for a higher price.

> **FOUL FACT**
>
> One Roman slave, called Daphnis, was sold at auction for 700,000 sesterces. This would buy you a brand new Jaguar car these days!

Primary Schools

Hiring private tutors was expensive, so most people sent their children to school. There was no state education system in ancient Rome. Teachers set up their schools wherever they could and this sometimes meant in the open air, perhaps under a tree. A more wealthy teacher might hold lessons in

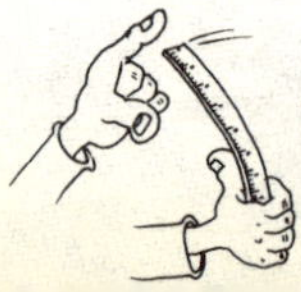

his own house. Some classes were given in the street, or in shops, or the market, called the "forum", which was the centre of town life.

The teachers were usually poor, as the rich did not send their children to schools and the poor could not afford to pay very much for education.

Now, in case you were wondering what the average Roman school day was like:

A Day in the Life of Fredus Bloggus, Pompeii, 50 BC

Marsday, The Ides of March
Got up before cock-crow. Felt tired so made my slave Obsequius Genuflectus carry me to school. Bought breakfast from the Baker's on the way.

Went into class and greeted my Master, Vilus Brutus. Still dark so had to light oil lamp.
Master put me in charge of group of younger children, including Wettus Beddus. Perfect.
Got young kids chanting alphabet forwards and backwards. Boring. Thinks: why do Masters always wear old togas with leather patches? Bench v. hard. Wish we had chairs so I could go to sleep.
Just then Master came past and gave me clip round ear-hole with ferule for dozing off.

Clumsius Prattus knocked my arm and book unrolled. It's the Master's only book, so I wasn't popular. Got another clip for that. Will sort Clumsius out tomorrow.

Told young kids to do some writing. Some had no wax on tablets, others had lost tablets, rest had left stilus at home.

Typical! Tried to do some finished work on papyrus, but cuttlefish was dry so couldn't get any ink. Wish someone would invent ball-points.

Good punch-up during Break. Julius Caesar supporters versus Pompey supporters. Don't know what we'll do for a laugh when the Civil War ends.

Maths after break. Got younger kids chanting multiplication tables. Then did some calculus, counting pebbles, but dropped some, so wrote down ix + vi = xii. Had to write out 25 times, "Work Hard, boy, lest you be thrashed!" Master in lousy mood and kept muttering that we shouldn't be allowed to use a Personal Abacus, we'd never learn how to calculate properly…
Sports in the afternoon…

Class orders out this afternoon. Why am I never top? It's not fair. This month it was:

1-Teachus Pettus
2-Servilius Creepus
3-Phonus Bolonus
4-Squeacus Cleanus
5-Mardius Cattus
6-Lostus Homworcus
7-Euslus Gittus
8-Daftus Abrushus
9-Fredus Bloggus
10-Thicus Abricus (AGAIN!)

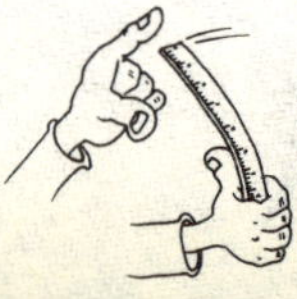

FOUL FACTS GUIDE TO SURVIVING SCHOOL

Well, you may be saying to yourselves, it's all very interesting finding out what Fredus Bloggus got up to, but what about MODERN TIMES? Will this book help ME with school? OF COURSE!

You've got to go to school. You might not want to, BUT it's the law. If you don't go, your Mum and Dad can get fined. So, since you've got to go, you might as well make the best of it. This handy guide will help you to overcome some of the problems you might find.

Schools are full of important people. Try to get on with them.

FRIENDS

Make some, but choose ones that don't bully you, get you to do their homework or nick all your sweets. These are not proper friends…
Proper friends do what you say, do your homework and give you sweets…. The one trouble is that, if they've read this book, they'll probably be avoiding you!

SCHOOL CARETAKERS

Forget head teachers, teachers, governors, etc! Caretakers are the people who really run the school.

They can make sure that classrooms are open (or closed), hot or cold. Ever been in a room where it was either too hot or too cold? No doubt the caretaker didn't like whoever was teaching in that room and turned the radiator off out of spite.

Caretakers are also known as Premises Officers or Site Managers or, occasionally, "O Mighty One". They used to be called janitors (doorkeepers), but now realize what great power they have. Even head teachers fear caretakers. **DO NOT GET IN THEIR BAD BOOKS!**

SCHOOL DINNER LADIES

Also important people. They can make sure that you get lots of food or none at all. A little courtesy costs nothing, and could bring you extra custard and chips for life. On the other hand, call a school dinner lady a sour-faced old ratbag and you'll probably get custard ON your chips, and serve you right!

SECRETARIES

Very important people. Get on their good side as they will let you sit in the medical room if you want to skive a lesson. They can also "lose" your phone number when a teacher asks them for it in order to ring up your parents to complain about you.

Teachers always need to keep secretaries sweet, because they always want something typed up immediately. So stick to your friendly secretary like glue when your teacher is on the warpath, and (s)he won't dare touch you!

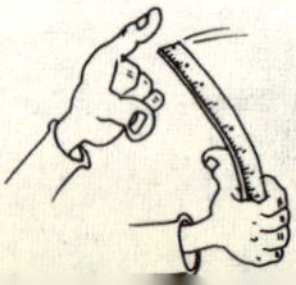

Those are the really important people. Others you meet are just a fact of life. For instance:

TEACHERS

Teachers are like spots – part of growing up and very annoying! Just put up with them. Like you, they probably don't want to be at school either. They'd rather be at home, at the pub or lying on a beach.

A question to ask your teachers:
Why are you a teacher? They will most likely give one of these answers:

a) The holidays are good.
b) I like teaching.
c) The money is good.

If a teacher answers b or c,(s)he is probably lying!

BULLIES

These are a nasty fact of life. Do not put up with them at all. Inform a teacher or your parents if there is bullying happening.

Some people may accuse you of "grassing people" up when you report bullies. You will notice that the only people who do this are the bullies themselves.

If YOU are a bully, what's your problem and why do you have to pick on your fellow pupils? Are you such a sad act that you can only feel good by making other people miserable? Get a life!

THE ART OF THE ABSENCE NOTE

Only a complete maniac would expect you to rot away in a classroom every day of the school year. Unfortunately, such maniacs include all your teachers, your parents and the Secretary of State for Education. That's why the Art of the Absence Note is the most important skill to acquire for surviving in the Whiteboard Jungle of modern schools. Here are two examples of sick notes, showing HOW NOT TO DO IT and HOW TO DO IT RIGHT.

HOW NOT TO DO IT

WRONG – your parents will never know your teacher's name. This is a dead giveaway before you even start.

WRONG – NEVER DATE A SICK NOTE. You may want to use it again.

WRONG – your parents don't care about your teacher's health. They don't even care about YOUR health, for Pete's sake, or they'd believe you when you tell them you're ill and you wouldn't have to forge notes in the first place.

8th May

Dear Mrs Phelps,

I hope you are well.

Unfortunately, our son Fred is suffering from chicken pox. He wanted so much to come in to school today. He begged me to let him get up as he was so looking forward to his maths test, but he has a high temperature and the doctor told him to stay in bed all day. Don't bother to send any work home for Fred. He will be much too ill to do it. I expect to be back at school next week.

Your humble and obedient servant

WRONG – much too easy to check when you get back. Avoid anything with spots. Never use bandages on bogus injuries: this is really naff.

WRONG – don't overdo it. A bit of creeping is OK, but there are limits.

WRONG – parents would never say this. They always ask teachers to send you work to do at home. But don't worry! Teachers never actually remember to make sure that you've done it.

WRONG – a dead giveaway. One slip and you're cat meat, so read your forgery over carefully.

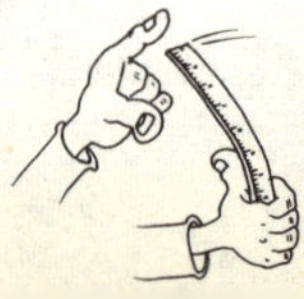

HOW TO DO IT RIGHT

Dear Teacher,

My son Fred is very sick. The doctor says this is a result of overwork and too much standing around on freezing playing fields, cold showers etc.

In his weakened state he has caught ophiothrix fragilis, which as you know can be very serious. Though there are no physical signs of this disease, people who suffer from it just get very tired all the time. In fact, even when Fred returns to school, the doctor says it is probable that he will frequently lay his head on his desk and go to sleep.

Sufferers from this disease become very nervous. It is vital that nobody should shout at Fred or give him any punishments, as this could easily make his condition worse.

Due to the highly contagious nature of his illness I am keeping Fred in quarantine and I have taken the phone off the hook to prevent any loud noises from disturbing him.

I hope Fred will be able to return to school in the foreseeable future.

Yours sincerely
Emily Bloggs (Mrs)

BRILLIANT! This will make your teacher feel guilty. (S)he will also start worrying about being sued for brutality, hindering your development etc.

This is actually the Latin name for a species of starfish, but never mind! Your teacher won't know that unless (s)he's a marine biologist. If this is the case, claim to have Blackthorne's Disease. By the time your teacher has discovered there's no such thing, you'll have thought of something else.

Clever! You've not only covered yourself for this absence, but you can also blame dozing off in class on your medical condition...

...and what's more, your teacher won't even dare to shout at you about this or anything else!

Or to put it another way, don't bother phoning to check up.

We think this is probably vague enough. It shows that your parents think your schooling is important but it doesn't commit you to anything.

THE TOP TEN EXCUSES FOR BEING LATE

Guaranteed to work or your money back!*

1. **The car broke down.**
   Don't mention that you never come to school in a car.
2. **The bus was late.**
   Don't mention that you live next door to the school.
3. **I was staying at my grandmother's/grandfather's/ aunty's/uncle's/cousin's or with any other distant relative.**
   Don't explain WHY this should have made you late. Just say it confidently and act as though the teacher should understand.
4. **My goldfish/dog/cat/parrot/beetle has died.**
   You may of course name any animal. This excuse will get sympathy from the teacher and has been known to get pupils off lessons all day. Try to have a few tears in your eyes – peel an onion just before you go into class.
   WARNING: Don't use this excuse too many times as the RSPCA will be round wanting to know why your pets keep dying.
5. **I had to take my sister/brother to school.**
   Don't mention that they are older than you and work in a bank.
6. **Mum/Dad didn't set the alarm clock.**
   Some teachers may ask why your parents should set YOUR alarm clock when it's next to YOUR bed. Ignore this sarcasm.

** Actually, this is a lie. All teachers know the above excuses. In fact, they almost certainly used them themselves when they were pupils, so they probably won't work. Anyway, what money?*

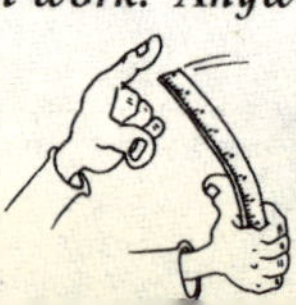

7. **There was a power cut last night.**
   Teachers will assume that your electric alarm clock failed. Don't tell them that you have a wind-up Mickey Mouse one.
8. **I forgot my homework so I had to go back and get it, but Mum had already gone out when I got back home.**
   This is a good one if you are supposed to be handing in some homework. Not only does it give you a good excuse for being late. It also makes it sound as though you have done your homework.
9. **There was a dinosaur/alien being/escaped tiger rampaging up the street.**
   This is just as likely to work as anything else, because teachers won't believe you, no matter what you say.
10. **Sorry I'm late but it started last night when Mum forgot to set my alarm. Then the dog died and there was a power cut so I had to stay at my grandmother's, but the car broke down and the bus was late so I had to take my brother to school. Then I forgot my homework so I had to go back, but mum was out and, on the way back, there was a dinosaur trying to eat everyone and that's why I'm late.**
    Your teacher will be so fed up and bored by the time that you are half way through the story that (s)he will just tell you to shut up, sit down, get on with your work and don't be late again.

TEN ROTTEN EXCUSES FOR NOT DOING YOUR HOMEWORK

If you have ever used, or are thinking of using, any of the following excuses, we are wasting our time trying to teach you. You are clearly a hopeless amateur and will probably end up as a traffic warden or a TV game show host.

1. **I've done it, honestly, but I've left it at home.**
   This is the worst excuse ever! No teacher is going to fall for this one.
2. **The dog/cat ate it.**
   How many dogs/cats would ever eat a book? "Nine out of ten owners said that their cat prefers paper to cat food"?! We think not.
3. **Homework? What homework? You never set us any homework, did you?**
   Yes, of course they did. All teachers set homework at the slightest opportunity.
4. **My baby brother spilt milk on it and so I put it to dry in front of the fire, but then I forgot about it and it got burnt.**
   You have got to be joking! This one is as old as the hills. Do you train your brother to throw milk over your books?
5. **I thought you said it had to be in NEXT Monday.**
   So why has everyone else in the class completed the homework THIS Monday?
6. **I've been ill.**
   Therefore you've been at home, so you've had more time to do it.
7. **I've left it at my grandmother's/grandfather's etc.**
   How many people take their homework with them when they visit relatives? Correct: none!

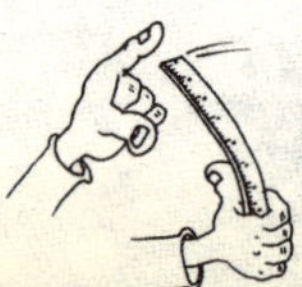

8. **I didn't understand it, so I couldn't do it.**
   "Okay, so you can stay every breaktime/ lunchtime/after school for the next year and I'll explain it to you."
9. **I dropped it in a puddle on the way to school.**
   "So show me the book" or "It hasn't rained for a week, so where did the puddle come from?"
10. **I haven't done it.**
    The honest answer, but the one that will cause any teacher to go into a mega go-through-the-ceiling-into-space-and-out-of-the-universe shouting tantrum at you.

Now turn the page to find out what we know (the author's that is) about education in the Dark Ages.

School

It was around this time that someone had an idea about chalkboards...

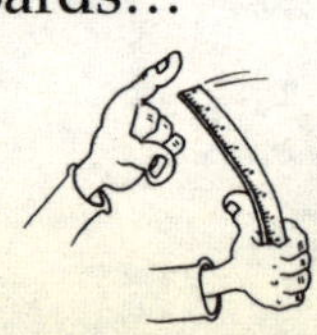

SCHOOL DINNERS

Have school dinners changed over the years? See what you think!

EARLY SCHOOL DINNERS

In **Roman** schools, dinners were evidently no better than they are today. Diogenes taught his pupils to "wait upon themselves and be content with plain fare and drink".

TUDOR MEALS

Beef and mutton; bread and beer;* and, on fishdays, eggs, milk and butter.

* In fact, lots of beer! But before anyone starts cheering, bear in mind that Tudor beer probably tasted like fish widdle. The only reason people drank it was that it was safe compared to the water supply, most of which had things dying in it.

The Tudor equivalent of tomato ketchup was mustard. It was smothered over food to disguise the taste when it was not very fresh.

VICTORIAN DINNERS

In *Nicholas Nickleby*, Charles Dickens tells us everything we need to know about meals in Victorian schools. The pupils of Wackford Squeers at "Dotheboys Hall" are dosed first of all with brimstone (sulphur) and treacle. Mrs Squeers says this is "partly because if they hadn't something or other in the way of medicine they'd be always ailing and giving a world of trouble, and partly because it spoils their appetities and comes cheaper than breakfast and dinner". These are their meals:

BREAKFAST:	thin brown porridge; a tiny square of brown bread
LUNCH:	hard salt beef (to know what this tastes like, try eating an old shoe)
SUPPER:	bread and cheese

MODERN DINNERS

A few years ago, school dinner menus were put together by experts in nutrition. Their job was to make sure that all school children got a healthy balanced diet. It may have tasted like old socks, but at least you knew it was HEALTHY.

These days, it's difficult sometimes to tell the difference between the school canteen and your local burger bar.

THE EVOLUTION OF SCHOOL DINNER LADIES

5000 BS

MODERN TIMES

MEDIEVAL SCHOOLS

Teachin' Preachin'...

Priests in medieval English churches had a slight problem. The Church of England didn't yet exist, and the Catholic Church was run by Rome. Because of this, all church services and all Bibles were in Latin. In fact, Latin was the language used for almost all books of this time. Priests were often the only educated members of a community. Therefore, schools in the Middle Ages were run by them and to begin with everything was taught in Latin. In the best schools, pupils were expected to speak Latin all the time.

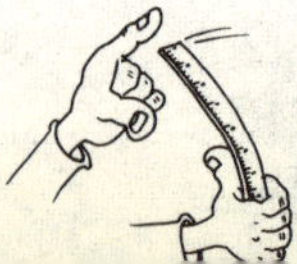

Priests were all supposed to have gone to school, but, in fact, many were ignorant and illiterate. They memorized lessons (usually incorrectly) and chanted them parrot-fashion.

ANOTHER FOUL FACTUS

Robert Grosseteste *, Bishop of Lincoln ** and winner of the All-Time-Silliest-Name-For-A-Bishop Competition, often had to refuse to allow complete dunces into the church. Many would-be teachers who came to him were lazy or useless, rich men's sons who just wanted a cushy job.

* This is French for "horrible exam".°

** There's a teacher training college in Lincoln named after Bishop Grosseteste.°°

° This is not true.

°° This is true.

Foul Medieval Teachers

The trouble with teaching in the Middle Ages was that teachers weren't very highly regarded, or very well paid (no change there!) Schools advertised for teachers with Masters degrees, but many teachers, even in fashionable schools, had no degree at all.

Most important people were more concerned about finding a good groom for their horses than about getting a good teacher for their children.

Classroom Crooks

Some teachers were real villains (no change there, again!) For example, **Henry,** the schoolmaster at Huntingdon in 1255, and his assistant Robert were convicted poachers.

School

Reginald, a schoolmaster of Norham, was involved in a punch-up in 1302. A monk was dragged by his feet out of Auckland parish church and beaten up. Beating someone up INSIDE a church was bad manners and against the Law of Sanctuary.

AN ABSOLUTELY DISGUSTING FOUL FACT

School lavatories in the Middle Ages were often Earth Closets (in other words, a hole in the ground) but some thrifty schools had their pupils pee in buckets, which would be carried away from time to time by one of the poor children at the school: the collected widdle would be bought by dyers and tanners, who used it to make the ammonia they needed to cure and dye leather. "For 'other causes', if need be," one schoolmaster of the time remarked, "they shall go to the waterside."

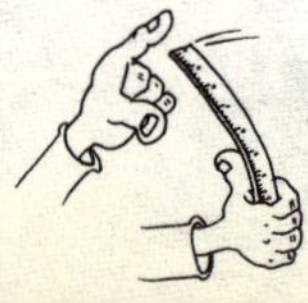

John Martyn of Oxford employed his pupils as a sort of gang, to help him in his evil-doing. Once, fearing that the parish priest was about to excommunicate him (throw him out of the church), Martyn gathered a number of pupils in the church at Mass, ready to drag the clergyman from his pulpit if he dared to try it. On another occasion a group of his students tried to rescue him from the town's jail! No wonder people said: "Lorde god, howe many goode and clene *wittes* (minds) of children be nowe a days *perisshed* (spoilt) by ignorant school maistres."

Who Needs School?

The Nobility

Medieval nobles (knights, etc) mostly needed to know how to knock the stuffing out of each other, and so they learned to ride and to fight. However, they also had to govern their estates in peacetime, and therefore they took reading and writing lessons. They didn't fancy them much. One irate father complained:

I swear by God's body I'd rather my son should hang than study letters.

The Middle Classes

Lawyers and civil servants needed to know Latin, but it wasn't so important for merchants and craftsmen. Most everyday business was carried out in either English or French, which had been the language of the upper classes since the Norman Conquest. Anyone who wanted to learn a trade had to be apprenticed to a craftsman. By the mid-15th century apprentices were usually taught to read and write at Business Schools.

The Villeins

Otherwise known as peasants, the villeins were practically slaves. They couldn't send their sons to school, without permission from the Lord of the Manor. The fear was that an educated villein might leave the manor and be difficult or expensive to replace. A licence to allow a boy to be taught could cost as much as twenty shillings, a fortune in those days!

Women

Women weren't allowed in schools. Nuns were the only women who could hope for any kind of education, and even they weren't expected to understand Latin. Wives and daughters of the nobility might learn to read, so that they could understand religious books and poetry, but hardly any of them could write well.

Primary Schools

These took pupils from seven to ten years of age. They were run by cathedrals and large churches and were called "Reading" or "Song" schools. Reading

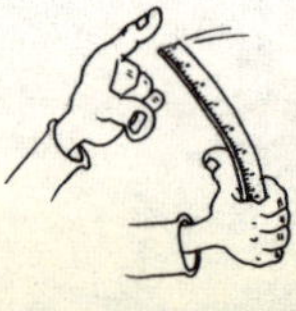

was always done aloud and singing was important. Reading was learnt from "primers", small books of mostly religious writings and prayers. Children would learn the words of songs in Latin, without understanding what they meant.

Schools of Higher Study

These taught the "Seven Liberal Arts", church law and theology. The greatest of these schools flourished at Oxford and Cambridge and became the first Universities.

In between these and the primary schools there were the…

Grammar Schools

Most large towns had one. They were the equivalent of modern secondary schools. Pupils started at any age between nine and twelve. The schools charged fees and took boarders, so that children from the country could attend.

Public Schools

These were more expensive than grammar schools.

Only rich people could afford to send their children there.

Grizzly Grammar

The idea of spelling in the Middle Ages was that you took a running shot at it and trusted to luck. There was no "correct" way of spelling words until much later. On the other hand, rules of grammar were very strict:

> *"How many are the parts of speech?*
> *Eight.*
> *What are they?*
> *Noun, pronoun, verb, adverb, participle, conjunction, preposition, interjection.*
> *What is a noun?*
> *A part of speech with a case, properly or commonly signifying a body or thing.*
> *How many characteristics have nouns?*
> *Six.*
> *What are they?*
> *Quality, comparison, gender, number, form and case."*

Have you got all that? Me neither!

The Alphabet

For pupils in the 14th century, the alphabet was usually written up in black paint on the whitewashed classroom wall. Alternatively, it was carved on a piece of wood, covered with a transparent piece of horn. This made a "hornbook". The alphabet looked like this:

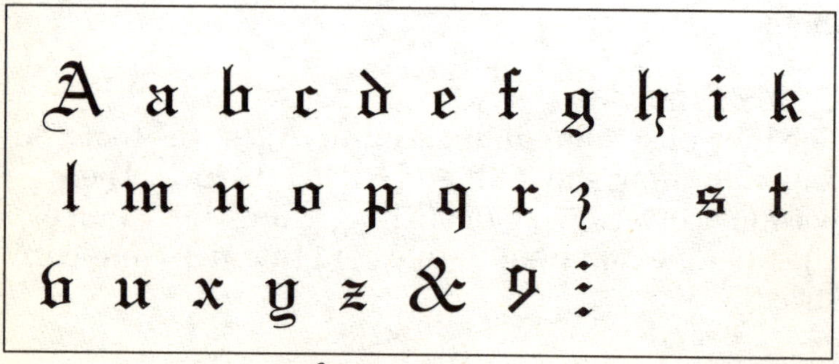

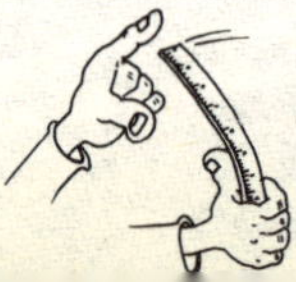

A Daye in the Lyfe of Mafter Fredericke Blogges, London, AD 1450

I rose at firste crowe of the Coke (6 am) and sayde my morning prayeres.

First classe at 7am (Latyne: I hayte Latyne).

More prayeres. My prayere ys, O God, let us notte have Gruel for breakfaste this morning. Breakfaste at 8 am: Gruel.

My Mastere wanted to see me; he seyde, "Blogges, your faythere has notte payde 8 pence for your schoolinge this yeare; I onelie have sixety-four studentes. Howe am I supposede to mayke a livinge?"

I sayde I wold wryte to my faythere and aske him to sende the monnaye (realy he has already sente it; I spent it on a newe doublette laste weeke, for my olde jackete was welle oute of dayte, my classemates were startinge to calle me a scruffe).

Classese start at 10 am. That littele swotte Thos Mallory wantede to borrowe a penne. I tolde him to naffe off and buy his owne pens. He sayde he was writinge a historie of the Deathe of Kinge Arthure onlie his penne hadde buste, I sayde toughe.

My Mastere has no assistant atte presente, so taughte us alle from his high chaire while we satte on our formes and scribbled.

More Latyne (I hayte Latyne); I hadde to translayte into Latyne this sentence; "The blinde manne eateth many a fly." Whatte is thatte supposed to meane? Yesterdaye yt was "Neede maykethe the olde wyfe to trot." Our Mastere sayes these sentences are callede "Vulgaria"- dead Vulgaria if you aske me.

My brothere, Blogges Major, was excusede fyve mynites earlie as hys wyfe hadde to goe oute; thys is notte fayre. I do notte thynke it ryte for pupilse toe have wyves and childrene at home, especially when they gette to skyve offe.

Atte Noone (12 o'cloke) we hadde dinnere.
Alle afeternoone we learnte Gramere (I hayte Gramere) untile 4 o'cloke when we playde Ball, thirtye-two a syde; yt is a greate gayme with lottes of fyghtinge. Sympkyne Mynor was carryde off ande I here hys lyfe is despaird of. I bette some boringe olde foole wille invent some rules for the game some daye and spoyle ytte. *
Atte 5 pm we hadde more prayeres and wente home. Rolle on the holydays - Shrove Tuesday nexte, we are allowde Coke-fyghtinge. I lyke Coke fyghtinge but I do notte thynke it fayre that the Cokes that lose shoulde be eaten by the Mastere.

**NB This game is still played at Ashbourne in Derbyshire.*

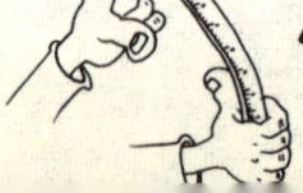

FOUL FACTS OF WORLD EDUCATION

Do you spend more time sitting gazing out of the window and picking your nose than you do writing? The answer is probably "yes", but we say STOP FEELING SORRY FOR YOURSELF!

If you are reading this book, then be thankful. There are millions of people in the world who are illiterate: they cannot read or write. This is usually because the countries they live in are so poor that they cannot provide schools. Either that or the people of the country are too busy trying to survive to have any time for learning. And you moan about homework!

The countries with the largest numbers of illiterate people are:

1 India	281 MILLION people
2 China	224 MILLION people

In other countries, with smaller populations, very large proportions of those populations cannot read or write:

Burkino Faso	81.8%
Sierra Leone	79.3%
Benin	76.6%
Guinea	76.0%
Somalia	75.9%

School

Nepal (Asia)	74.4%
Sudan	72.9%
Gambia	72.8%
Niger	71.6%

EDUCATION IN OTHER COUNTRIES

There are many types of educational systems around the world. Can you identify which country's education system is being described? (Answers on next page.)

Country A

- There are 750,000 schools.
- 150,000,000 students.
- Compulsory education for 5 years.
- The main school holidays are usually taken in May and June.
- Pupils have to attend school six days a week.
- The primary education aims to promote *Positive attitudes towards human labour and responsibility to the self and others.*
- By the end of secondary education, students must know the principles of democracy, secularism and socialism.

Country B

- There are 41,000 schools.
- There are 20,000,000 students.
- Education is compulsory for 5-15 year-olds.
- Students have to attend school on weekdays and Saturday mornings.
- Exams are VERY important.
- Holidays are usually taken in July and August.
- The PE programme includes martial arts.

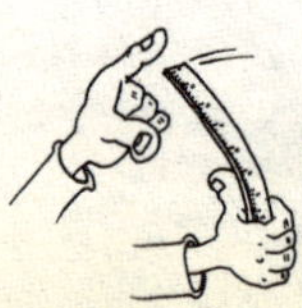

Country C

- There are 10,000 schools.
- There are 3,750,000 students.
- Education is compulsory for 6-16 year-olds (although this varies slightly from state to state).
- Summer holidays are taken in December and January.
- Students study similar subjects to those studied in the UK.

FOUL JAPANESE FACTS

Exam Hell! In Japan, exams are so important that many Japanese kids go to special private schools to revise for them. These schools are called JUKU. It is considered a total disgrace for students to fail their exams as they will not be able to gain good jobs. The system is sometimes called JUKEN JIGOKU, which means "examination hell".

Alphabet Hell! By the age of 15, Japanese students must have learnt to write all of the Kanji. These are the characters that make up the alphabet. Unfortunately for the poor Japanese students, there are 1,945 characters!

ANSWERS: A INDIA, B JAPAN, C AUSTRALIA

TUDOR AND ELIZABETHAN SCHOOLS

In Tudor times schools went through an incredible change. This was mainly due to King Henry VIII (the one who had six wives).

At the beginning of Henry's reign, schools were toddling along as they had done in the Middle Ages. The Church provided much of the education, in monasteries and Church schools. But then Henry had a MEGA BIG disagreement with the Pope, the head of the Catholic Church, about whom he could and couldn't marry. (Henry, that is, not the Pope. The

Pope can't get married – perks of the job, we suppose). Henry decided that he could do without the Pope. He set up the Church of England and declared that he was the head of it, so yah boo sucks!

One result of all this was that Henry closed down all the monasteries in England – and pinched most of the Church lands in 1548. And, of course, this meant that most of the elementary schools were closed down too. Only a few grammar schools were left. Most of these became known as King's schools.

What a brilliant King! Any chance of this happening again today?

A COPY-OUT-AND-SEND FOUL FACTS LETTER

To HRH Prince Charles
c/o Buckingham Palace
London E II R

Dear Prince Charles,
When you are King, could you please close down the schools like your great-great-great-great (and a lot more greats) grandad Henry VIII did?
Thank you very much.
Your loyal subject (very loyal if you pull this stunt off)

(Sign your name)

PS In the meantime, don't send William and Harry to

.... (Insert the name of your school).

It's a dump.

Education for Girls

When Henry shut down the monasteries and kicked out the monks, he also closed the nunneries. History doesn't tell us whether he kicked out the nuns too, but a man who had two of his wives' heads chopped off obviously wouldn't muck about. The closing of the nunneries put an end to the little education that girls had been getting.

> **A HENERY OF A FOUL FACT**
> In 1540, Henry VIII ordered all schools to follow two standard grammar books and banned all others – in other words, he invented the first National Curriculum!

Grammar Schools

To make up for closing down the Church schools, Henry VIII and his successors Edward VI, Mary I and Elizabeth I set up many grammar schools. Thanks a heap, gang!

FOUL FACTS QUICK QUIZ
TICK THE SCHOOLS YOU THINK WERE FOUNDED IN TUDOR TIMES (1485-1603). (Answers on next page.)

- Shrewsbury
- Eton College
- Repton
- Rugby
- Queen Mary's School for Girls
- Uppingham
- Harrow
- Blog Street Comprehensive
- Leeds Grammar School
- Gordonstoun

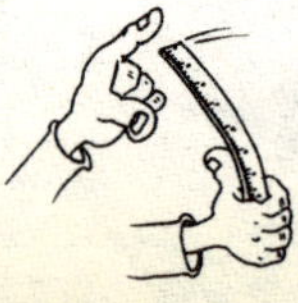

In fact, so many grammar schools were founded that no boy lived more than 12 miles from a grammar school where he could obtain a free education – or so it was said! Many schools were "free", but students had to pay an admission fee. Many children did not attend schools because they had to work instead.

OTHER SORTS OF TUDOR SCHOOLS

Petty Schools

Many grammar schools would only admit pupils who could already read and write. To prepare themselves for grammar school, boys between 6 and 8 years old went to petty schools. They were called this because they were for small children (from the French word "petit").

Dame Schools

At these schools children up to the age of 7 were supposed to learn reading and writing, but other skills such as knitting and spinning were also taught – usually by elderly women (hence the name "dame

QUICK QUIZ ANSWERS: All of them except for Blog Street Comprehensive, Queen Mary's School for Girls, Eton College (1440) and Gordonstoun (where Prince Charles went) which was founded in 1934.

schools"). The brighter pupils (or the ones who could afford it) might go on to grammar schools.

Trade Schools

These were set up to teach trades like printing, accounting, shoemaking and weaving. They were also known as "craft schools". No, we said "cra**FT** schools". Please stop giggling and pay attention. They were very like the vocational schools that the government is trying to set up at the moment. Teachers were paid little, and standards weren't high.

Universities

Pupils who could afford to went on to either Oxford or Cambridge University. The minimum age was supposed to be 15, but this was often ignored. Many students were under 14. The Second Earl of Essex was 10 when he went to Cambridge!

Public Schools and Private Schools

Most of these weren't affected by Henry's quarrels with the Church and just carried on as usual. There

was a good deal of rivalry between these older schools and the new grammar schools.

Now let us move on swiftly and examine how Elizabethan Blog spent much of his time.

A Day in the Lyfe of Young Frederick Blogg Esquire, Stratforde upon Avon, 1584

Before dawn
Got up and had to walk to school. I would have waited for a school bus but it won't be along for another 500 years and I'd get a real beating for being THAT late.
Passed Anne Hathaway's cottage. I waved at her but she ignored me. She has the Hottes for that little Swotte Will. Shakespeare.

Six of the cloke
Arrived at school. I wish it was winter. Although the weather is worse than summer, at least we don't start until 7 o cloke. Said Prayers. I prayed that I wouldn't get another beating today. Unfortunately I was so busy praying that I didn't notice everyone else had started class and I got a beating for not paying attention. This proves that there is No Justice.

Latin. Read an amusing tale about a hare and a strange animal called a tortoise by a man called Aesop. They had a race, and the hare was winning, but he lay down for a nappe and the tortoise won the race – but then its owner put it in an airing cupboard where it dyed. The moral is, it's not much fun being a tortoise.

Eight of the cloke
Grammar. I wrote a play called "Omlet, the Potty Prince of Dorset." It had lots of ghosts and murders and I thought it was dead goode but the master gave me a beating and F minus as we were supposed to be doing a comprehension. The creepe Will. Shakespeare said he liked the idea, did I mind if he had a looke at it and changed a few names? I said he could do what he liked with it, if he wanted to waste his time, I had to go for a pee. He muttered, "To pee, or not to pee," and wandered off looking thoughtful. Twerp!

Nine of the cloke
Prayers before breakfast. Bread and butter again! Still, it's better than those potato things Sir Walter Raleigh brought back from America. My Aunt gave me some last time I was in London. Yeuch! Take it from me, they'll never catch on. After breakfast, Religious instruction followed by more prayers.

Twelve of the cloke
Yet more prayers, then dinner time.
Tried to sneak off to the tavern for a mug of ale and to try out the new fashion. It is called tobacco: you set fire to it and breathe it in. (Honestly!) Got caught and received another beating.

One in the afternoon
More prayers. Surprise surprise!
During Geography, I found out the reason that John the Smith's son is not at school today. He is getting married. He is 12 years old which is a good age for marriage although his bride is young – she is 9.

Two in the afternoon
French. Tres boring. I told Will. Shakespeare one of my dad's jokes. Unfortunately the master heard me and I got another beating.

Half past Three of the Cloke
An intermission. We should have more of these!

Four of the Cloke
Another beating for not speaking in Latin to Will. Shakespeare. He was telling me how he was going to London to become a famous playwright, I said don't be daft, you haven't even been to public school.

Five of the cloke
Prayers and psalm singing. We also sang "Greensleeves" which we have sung every day for a year. I think it is a rotten songe but the Queen's dad wrote it so everybody has to sing it unless they want to carry their heads home in their schoolbags.

Six of the cloke
Began the walk home.

Eight of the cloke
*Bed. Wound up the bedside cockerel * and set it to wake me up at dawn.*

**How do you wind up a cockerel? Easy, you whisper "Who's a big hen, then?"*

FABULOUS FOUL FACT

In 1581, Queen Elizabeth I passed a law that said that if any school teacher didn't go to church on Sundays or Holy Days, he or she would be thrown into prison for a WHOLE YEAR!
Maybe this law could be reintroduced? That'd get rid of a few teachers...

STRATFORDE UPON AVON GRAMMAR SCHOOL 1584 SCHOOL REPORT

MOTTO: Brummies Ara Pest.

PUPIL: *MASTER FREDERICK BLOGG,*
SON OF FREDERICK BLOGG Esquire

Grammar	*A dolt! He thinks that grammar is the wife of his grandpa!*
Latin	*Stupidum!*
French	*Pas sur votre Nelly!*
Geography	*This boy is so stupid he doesn't even understand that the world is flat or that the Earth moves round the sun!*
Divinity (RE)	*I have always believed that God in his wisdom created all things, but that was before I met your son.*
English	*He would do better if he didn't spend all his time whispering with that idler Will.Shakespeare. Neither of them will ever amount to anything!*

R . Bisto, Master

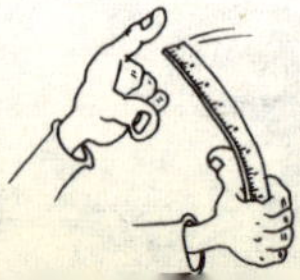

WOMEN'S EDUCATION

Right! We've spent a lot of time on the education of males. What about the education of girls? SEXIST MALE REPLY: Well, what about it? Unfortunately that has been the typical reaction throughout history!

In Britain, there wasn't much education for girls until the mid-17th century and, even then, there wasn't a lot! If you were poor, you could forget about it! If you were lucky enough to be born rich, you might get a home tutor or be sent to one of the very few private schools for girls that existed by the end of the 17th century. But, whether you were rich or poor, most people thought that the only decent career for a woman was – Marriage.

The problem was that some people didn't think that girls had the same right as boys to be educated. These people were (and in many cases still are) MEN!

FORMIDABLE FOUL FACTS

Lady Jane Grey (1537-54), who became Queen of England for a grand total of 14 days in 1553, had learnt French, English, Greek, Latin, Italian and Spanish before she was 6 and Hebrew, Chaldee and Arabic before she was 16!

Queen Elizabeth I spoke French, Spanish, Italian and Welsh and studied history for 3 hours a day.

School

Slowly schools for girls were introduced. They tended to be private educational establishments teaching the "lady-like" skills that their pupils would need to become good wives: dancing, drawing, sewing, music, writing letters, greeting people, sitting and standing "properly". These sorts of schools still exist. They are called finishing schools – presumably because, if you go there, your brain gets finished off very quickly!

QUICK LESSON QUIZ

In Victorian times girls were required to go to school, but they had a different set of lessons from boys. Guess who took which subjects.

LESSONS A	LESSONS B
Carpentry	Housewifery
Gardening	Sweeping
Farmwork	Dusting
Shoemaking	Making beds
Handicrafts	Bathing babies
	Needlework
	Cookery

ANSWER: Boys took Lessons A. Surprise! Surprise!

It was not considered normal for women to go on to higher education until quite late in the 20th century. Today there are still subjects which are seen as being "male", like engineering and computing, although things are slowly getting better.

UNJUST FOUL FACT

In most countries of the world more boys are sent to school than girls. The result is that there are more women than men who cannot read or write.

INTERMISSION: CAVALIERS, ROUNDHEADS AND SCHOOLS

Heads You Lose...

So what happened to education in the years from 1600 to 1800?
Not a lot! Oh, except that there was the English Civil War (1642-1649). The winners of the Civil War were Oliver Cromwell and the Puritans. They won the war by a head: King Charles I's head – they cut it off! And these Puritans were very interested in Education. One of their supporters, John Milton (a

dead famous English Poet – i.e. famous AND dead) thought that "reforming education" was "one of the greatest and noblest designs that can be thought on".

Many Puritans wanted free education for all, and their Parliament appointed new school masters. However, when Charles II was restored to the English throne in 1660, he got rid of this idea VERY quickly. He thought that too much schooling of the poor had caused the revolution against Charles I.

By this, of course, he meant that too much schooling of ordinary folk was bad for people like him and his aristocratic chums, who wanted to rule without anybody asking too many questions. They also didn't fancy having their heads chopped off like Charles I. Therefore Charles II banned extreme Puritans from being teachers – which was a great shame because a lot of them were very good. He also stopped the clock on the idea of free education for all, for another two hundred years.

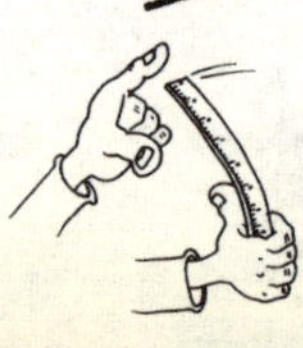

VICTORIAN EDUCATION

Victorian Benefactors?

We can thank the Victorians for many things:

Introducing tea to Britain
The Penny Farthing bicycle
The Penny Black postage stamp
Steam trains
Steel ships
Very long bridges
Some really awful poets and playwrights
AND
Compulsory schooling.

Yes, when you're sitting bored out of your head in some school lesson, you can thank the Victorians.

They introduced COMPULSORY FREE SCHOOLS for all children between the ages of 5 and 12. THANKS A LOT!

> **FOUL OXYMORONIC* QUESTION**
> **(*Look it up in a dictionary!)**
> **Who was the shortest and longest reigning monarch?**
> **Queen Victoria! She reigned from 1837 to 1901, but she was less than 1.5 metres (5 feet) tall.**

Many children didn't go to school at the beginning of the 19th century. They were too busy trying to earn money down mines, up chimneys, in factories or on farms. But during the reign of Queen Victoria it all changed!

AWFOUL LAWFOUL DATES

Try to decide whether the following were good or bad laws!

1833
National schools or British schools could apply for money from the government. This was the first time that the state gave money directly to help education.

1844
Children working in factories were to be given 6 half days of schooling every week.

1870
Fosters Education Act. All areas of the country had to provide schools for all 5-12 year-olds.

1880
School is made COMPULSORY for all 5-10 year-olds.

1891
Education is made free for all.

1899
School leaving age is raised to 12.

If you said "bad" each time, you obviously don't like school much!

VICTORIAN SCHOOL TYPES

A stupid question: Why were Sunday schools called Sunday schools?
The totally obvious answer: Because they were schools that took place on Sundays!

Sunday schools had already been around for a hundred years or more and were run by churches. In Victorian times some of them started to educate children on weekdays and became known as National or British schools.

Board Schools (or should that read BORED?)

These were set up after the 1870 Education Act, in places where there were no Church schools. They were also called elementary schools. They were run by committees (or boards) and paid for by local taxes and by charging pupils one penny a week.

School

Many children still didn't attend school, because they couldn't afford the penny or because they had to help their parents to earn money in order to survive.

Grammar Schools

Remember these had started off by being free schools? Well, times change and money talks. In Victorian times grammar schools charged fees, and so they were for the middle classes.

Public Schools

These were still around and still charging high fees. Mind you, paying loads didn't mean that you got a better education. Because the public schools, were so bad, the government ordered a big shake-up of them in 1868. It has been claimed that this shake-up has still not affected some modern-day public schools!

Ragged Schools

Ragged schools gave free education to poor children, in order to stop them becoming criminals. The teachers were volunteers and the funds came from

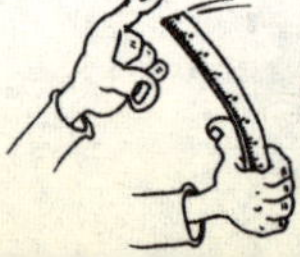

charities. These schools were for the shoeless, shirtless and capless.

DO-IT-YOURSELF SCHOOLING

Some board schools employed the PUPIL TEACHER system. Boys or girls over the age of 13 looked after the younger children. For this they were paid about 3 shillings (15p) a week.

This replaced the very bad MONITOR system, where a teacher taught the older children and they passed on what they knew to the younger ones and reported back to the teacher about their progress. By this method, there could be just one teacher for 500 pupils! But a lot of them didn't learn much at all, since many of the monitors couldn't read or write themselves.

CHANGES FOR THE BETTER?

1862: Teachers and schools are paid by results. The better the school and teacher do, the more money they receive.
1897: The "payment by results" system is abolished, as unfair and unjust.

1991: The government brings in the idea of paying teachers by results. The better they do, the more money they get...

THE THREE RS

The Victorians placed great importance on the "three 'Rs": Reading, Riting and Rithmetic. They obviously weren't too bothered about spelling!

FOWLDRAINS STREET ELEMENTARY SCHOOL, LONDON SCHOOL REPORT

MOTTO:	*Wotcha meold China.*
PUPIL:	*Freddie Bloggs.*
READING:	*He cannot read it.*
WRITING:	*I cannot read it.*
RITHMATIC:	*I cannot spell it.*

GENERAL REMARKS: *Unfortunately, because Bloggs has such low standards, he has not made the standard at this standard, and will not be able to move up to the next standard. This has also meant that my wages are going to be less, because of payment by results. Bloggs will also receive payment by results! I look forward to taking my anger out on him, or rather his backside. In other words, if he does not quickly make the standard, he will find it 'ard to stand!*

I. Wackum (Miss), Form Mistress

The Victorians were very keen on floggings, but they didn't invent them. For a Foul File on Pitiless Punishments, peruse the following pages!

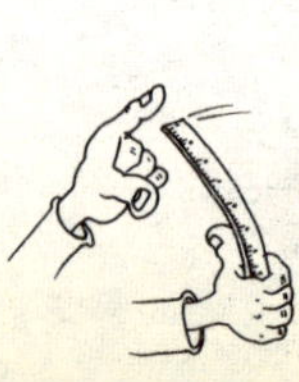

CRIMES AND PUNISHMENTS

Graffiti isn't a new problem. The earliest examples we know of were discovered on the wall of a villa in Pompeii, and on the Palatine building in Rome.

If you annoy Cicero, he'll beat you black and blue.

Work, you donkey, as I have worked, and much good may it do you!

Bunking Off

When a pupil called Persius wanted to avoid having to copy a difficult speech, he placed a few drops of olive oil in his eyes to make them water. Then he claimed that he could not see to read and was let off the exercise! Pretty clever, eh? Well, yes, but only as long as you don't get caught!

Throughout history, teachers have punished children for breaking school rules or misbehaving.

The Romans had some cruel instruments, as shown in our chart. When a Roman boy was whipped, he had to strip down to his loincloth (a type of jockstrap). One fellow pupil held him over his back, in a sort of piggy-back position, while another held his ankles. His back and buttocks were then given the treatment.

INSTRUMENT	MADE OF	SEVERITY
Ferule (Cane)	Stalk of Giant Fennel	
Scutica (Whip)	Strap with leather thongs on end	
Virgae (Rods)	Bundles of plant withies (twigs)	

Key:  nasty

 absolutely excruciating

 "Muuuummyyyyyy!!!!!"

The Tudors were brutal too, believing that beating was a good way of instilling discipline. Their chosen weapon was the birch. Beatings were given out even for offences such as:

Talking out of turn
Losing your school cap
Being late
Not attending church
Hanging around taverns

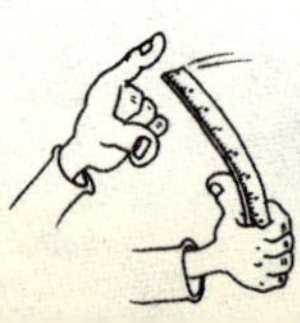

Deadly teacher!

The Elizabethan writer Thomas Ingelands claimed that a pupil was killed by his schoolmaster. The pupil was hung upside down by the heels and beaten before having his head crushed against the wall. This is an example of corporal punishment becoming capital.

Nicholas Udall, headmaster of Eton school in the 1530s, was known as "The Flogging Headmaster". He beat up to 70 pupils at a time, giving them as many as 60 strokes each. This laugh-a-minute man also wrote a famous play called *Ralph Roister Doister.* It is thought to be the first English comic play!

FOUL STRANGE-BUT-TRUE FACT!

Have you or your friends ever been punished for smoking? No, you don't smoke, we hear you say (very sensible). Well you could have been in BIG trouble in the 17th century. Tobacco was thought to keep the plague away and pipe-smoking was encouraged. At Eton in 1660 a schoolboy was beaten for NOT smoking!

The Victorians were the All-Time-Great World Experts on punishment. Like the Tudors, they thought that children should be beaten into behaving well. Here are a few of the rib-tickling punishments thought up by the Victorians. Pupils were:

Put in the stocks and left
Locked in a cupboard
Suspended from the roof in a basket
Handcuffed from behind
Forcibly washed in public
Strapped to a heavy piece of wood lashed across their shoulders
Made to wear a dunce's (fool's) cap

Any of these punishments were liable to be given for any of these offences:

Swearing
Lying
Playing truant
Arriving at school late
Arriving at school dirty
Telling tales
Being disobedient
Being absent from church

A Terrible Table of Victorian Viciousness

Compare this table to the chart of Roman punishments (see p 70) and see how little things changed in a couple of thousand years!

INSTRUMENT	MADE OF	SEVERITY
Tawse (Strap)	Hard leather	

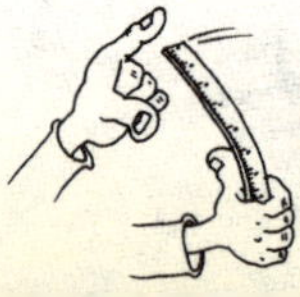

Rod (Cane)	Wood	
Birch (Whip)	Bundle of birch twigs	

Key:  agony

 crippling

 scarred for life

The tawse was invented in Scottish schools.

The rod was a sort of cane, but it was used for more severe beatings. Hence the expressions, "He's made a rod for his own back" and "Spare the rod and you'll spoil the child".

A rod could break during an especially harsh beating. To avoid such an inconvenience, conscientious Victorian teachers used to pickle their rods in vinegar (just as conkers are pickled today), which made them harder.

The birch was a bundle of birch twigs. It worked on the same principle as the cat o' nine tails, which was so popular in Nelson's navy. The principle is that being hit by several thin, hard, springy things at once is more painful than being hit by one thick, springy thing. The birch is still in use on the Isle of Man, and people who sign themselves *Disgusted of*

Tunbridge Wells would like to see it make a reappearance in mainland Britain.

> **A TOO-CLEVER FOUL FACT**
> It didn't pay to be too clever at Norwich Grammar School in the 1800s. The head, Dr Parr advised his teachers that they should flog the pupils if they showed any signs of being a genius!

The 20th Century

Corporal punishment in schools was still common in the civilized 20th century in Britain. The instruments of punishment included:

The slipper
The strap
The cane

Some politicians today say that they were beaten at school and claim it never did them any harm! Hmmm...!

THE END

The use of corporal punishment was finally banned in British state schools in 1986.

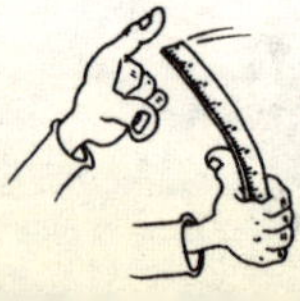

THE 20th CENTURY

The 20th century has seen great changes in society, and these have been reflected by great changes in education. At the beginning of the century, education had just been made free for all. Only 9% of 14 year-olds went to school. Today, the figure is 100%. Aren't you the lucky ones?

As we move towards the 21st century, there seems to be lots of upheaval in ideas about education. There have been great debates about the future of schools, who should control them, and what should be taught.

While there is no doubt that education has improved, some people are calling for a return to "old-fashioned standards". Some of them even think of bringing back schemes that the Victorians thought were bad! And call it progress! What do you think?

School

THEN

NOW

The Curriculum
$4^{1}/_{2}$ hours English, History, Geography
$3^{1}/_{2}$ hours Language
$7^{1}/_{2}$ hours Science & Maths

The Curriculum
English
History
Science
Language
Maths

Teaching Methods

Teaching Methods

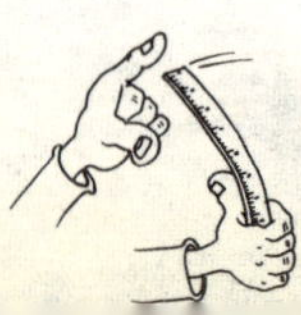

School Buildings

Exams
School Certificate
Higher school certificate

School Buildings

Exams
GCSEs / A Levels
GNVQs

THE FOUL FACTS HISTORY OF 20TH-CENTURY EDUCATION

1902: School boards abolished and Local Education Authorities (LEAs) set up.

This meant that education could be provided free for all children, including those over the school-leaving age of 12. Many new grammar schools were built as well as teacher training colleges.

1907: THE start of the 11 plus

All grammar schools were offered £5 per pupil if they took at least 25% of their pupils from local elementary schools. This led the grammar schools to find a method of selecting the more academically clever pupils they wanted, and the 11 plus exam was founded. If you didn't pass the exams, you stayed on at elementary school and studied more practical subjects.

YUCKY FOUL FACTS

Of the 6 million children at school in 1913:
3 million of them had bad teeth.
600,000 were "unclean of body" (i.e. they had stinkingly awful B.O. because they didn't wash very often).
120,000 had TB.
60,000 had ringworm.

1918: Up it goes!

The school-leaving age was raised again, this time to 14.

1939: Adolf stops school!

During the Second World War, schools closed down in large cities because of the fear of bombing. In fact, 1,150 of the 1,200 schools in London were damaged by bombs. Nearly 750,000 schoolchildren were evacuated to the countryside, in an operation called Operation Pied Piper. Many of the schools they moved to couldn't cope with the influx of so many children and had to teach them on a part-time basis.

1944: The Butler Education Act

This was nothing to do with the fact that British butlers weren't being taught to lay tables and serve soup properly. It is called the Butler Act because Mr Butler introduced it. His idea was to ensure equality of education for ALL.

All education in state-maintained grammar schools was to be free. Only children who passed the 11 plus could go to grammar schools.

All pupils were to leave primary schools at the age of 11. Secondary modern schools and technical

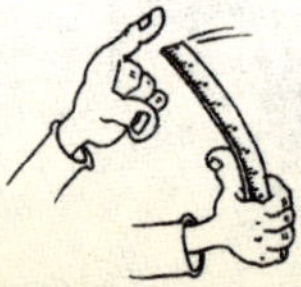

schools were set up for the pupils who failed the 11 plus.

Subsidized school meals were to be provided in every school. Free milk, a free medical service and a free dental service were also provided.

PS The school-leaving age was raised again, to 15.

1950s and 1960s: Goodbye 11 plus.

In the late 1950s and 1960s a new type of school was created – the comprehensive. This was because many people thought that the 11-plus system of education was unfair.

Comprehensive schools were for all pupils, of all abilities. Many grammar schools and secondary modern schools were changed into comprehensives. Today, most British children go to a comprehensive school.

1988: A new ERA (or, to give it its proper name, the Education Reform Act)

This is the act that is having the greatest effect on YOUR school life! It introduced the National Curriculum. Unfortunately, the first version of this Curriculum suggested that by the age of 11, a kid should be tested on nearly 2,000 different items, ranging from spelling to science. Of course, it was unworkable. Since then, the National Curriculum has gone through several changes in a very short time and it still isn't sorted out properly!

THE FOUL FACTS GUIDE TO SCHOOL SUBJECTS

MATHS

Maths is one of the foulest subjects ever known. There are several parts to it – all of them as foul as each other.

How Maths was invented (possibly)
It was invented by Archimedes – or was it Aristotle? Then again, it could have been Pythagoras – it's all Greeks to us.

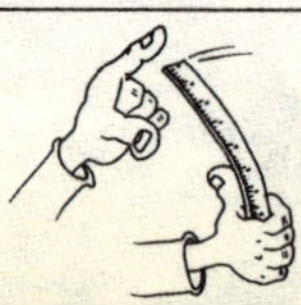

Anyway, Archimedes (or Aristotle or Pythagoras) was sitting in a bath thinking about mathematical problems. This proves that Archimedes (or Aristotle or Pythagoras) was a total nutso. Who thinks about Maths in the bath? It's bad enough having to think about Maths in a Maths lesson.

Things to do in a bath

Read comics or books
Play on a Gameboy
Pick scabs off knee
Wonder why belly fluff is always blue
Maybe wash

Things NOT to do in a bath

Think about Maths!

Suddenly, as Archimedes was thinking about maths, he realized the answer to the question that was puzzling him. He jumped out of the bath, shouted "Eureka" and ran stark naked round the town, getting some very strange looks indeed. If only he'd been arrested for indecent behaviour, millions of schoolkids would never have had to suffer Maths (possibly)!

WARNING: DO NOT copy ARCHIMEDES when you think of the correct answer in a Maths lesson. You would look very stupid running around the school with no clothes on and shouting "Eureka". You might also get a chill in places you aren't meant to.

PS Archimedes got his just reward. He was so busy thinking about another mathematical problem, that he ignored a Roman soldier who was talking to him. The Roman was annoyed at this and stabbed Archimedes to death to teach him a lesson. HA!

More mathematical misery...

GEOMETRY
Dictionary definition: A branch of Mathematics dealing with the relationships between points, lines, planes, figures, solids and surfaces.
Foul Facts definition: Boring work about stupid shapes.

STATISTICS
This involves lots of percentages. Politicians use statistics to prove whatever point they are trying to make. Then other politicians use the same statistics to prove the opposite point. Thus proving Mark Twain's comment: "There are lies, damned lies, and statistics."

ALGEBRA
Why do we have algebra? Who cares what X or Y equals? Do you? Nor do I. It has to be the most foul subject EVER!

ENGLISH

Wrightting iss veri impotent If u do knot know how to spill propurlee, yu wil nevur piss ani exshams and sirtaynlee nevur be a good wrightter or gett buks pubblishd licke what we doo. Puncktuashion! is allsow,! veri impotent" and if, you ca'n't't punk.tuate propiy then know won, [lick tee-churs) wil no wot! ew're". wrightting abowt'; so yu,ll nevur gett. gud marx:?!

Barlow and Skidmore, see me!
The Editor

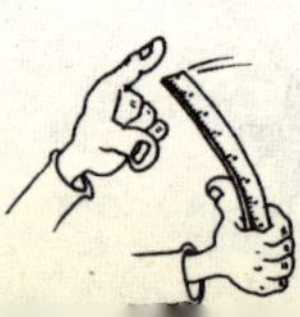

There are many exciting and funny books in the world (for example this one). Unfortunately, you are not usually allowed to read these at school. Instead, you are forced to read dead boring ones with stupid heroes and heroines called Lovelace Fancypants or Felicity Hairpiece, who say things like "La di dah", "Tush, my dear" and "Bless my soul".
The best thing to do is put up with these, read them, pretend they're the most amazing things ever written, so that your teacher will give you brill reports, and then read the good books at home.

DRAMA

A really doss subject. One of the good things about it is being able to thump your enemies and tell the drama teacher that it was all part of the play. This rather brilliant excuse can also be used when swinging from the stage lights, throwing furniture across the room, swearing at everyone and setting fire to the school theatre.

SCIENCE

As with Maths, there are several branches of Science. Sometimes schools lump them all together under the title SCIENCE. This is bad news, because, in our opinion, some science is good fun, while some is as boring as watching grass grow, paint dry or day-time television.

BIOLOGY

A very important subject. You get to find out about your bodies and, with a bit of luck, other people's bodies as well, which is a bit of a giggle. You also get to ask teachers very embarrassing questions.

CHEMISTRY
Chemistry can be good fun. You can learn how to blow up the school lab and make stink bombs.

BOTANY
Looking at flowers.

ASTRONOMY
Looking at stars.

PHYSICS
Looking at the clock, waiting for the lesson to end.

HISTORY

In History you have to learn dead boring or dead interesting facts about dead people.
Thanks to the National Curriculum, you will have to do a project on at least one of the following topics: The Romans, The Vikings, The Tudors, The Victorians, Britain in World War II, Spiderman Comics 1962-1992*.

GEOGRAPHY

Get a map of the world. Look at it. Remember where everything is. That's it, really.

ART

Another good doss subject. Splash a lot of paint around a bit of paper. When the teacher asks you what it is, say: "It's art. Surely you understand what it is." The teacher obviously won't have a clue (neither will you), but won't admit this and so will give it an A+. You can then sell the painting to the Tate Gallery for a million pounds, leave school and head for the Caribbean.

***This is a lie.**

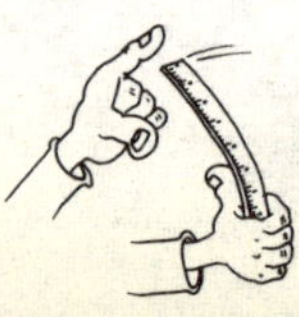

P.E.

Great fun if you like games and sports. If you don't, then having your finger nails ripped out is probably a more enjoyable option.

COMPUTERS (or INFORMATION TECHNOLOGY)

An essential subject if you want to learn how to commit robberies without leaving your home (i.e. by hacking into bank accounts, etc).
You can also play Sonic the Hedgehog 124, while pretending to work on important spreadsheets.

MUSIC

Great for making a noise! If your Music teacher tells you to keep the noise down, just say that you're trying to help him or her become like Beethoven (i.e. deaf!)

Most Music classrooms are miles away from the headteacher's office. Still, it's worth banging a drum or turning up a keyboard full blast to give the head a chance to hear your musical talents. You never know, you might be discovered.

FRENCH

Un tres importante subject, nes pas? Now we are dans Europe et aussi have le tunnel de Channel le Francais is tres tres essential.

WOODWORK

The greatest doss subject ever invented! If you play it right, you can take up to a year to finish a dovetail joint. When the teacher demands to know why you are taking so long, just say: "You can't rush a craftsman – look at Chippendale." This will shut up any self-respecting Woodwork teacher.

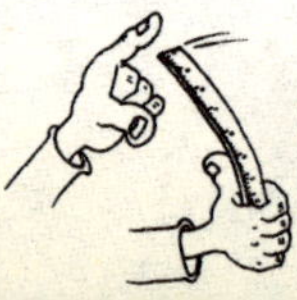

SCHOOL REPORTS

Everyone gets them. Nobody understands them, and usually this is just as well. The fact is that school reports are written in a sort of code. At great personal risk, Barlow and Skidmore have penetrated the Forbidden Staffroom to bring you information from the secret School Report Code Book.

WHAT THEY SAY	WHAT THEY MEAN
Is a quiet member of the class.	I don't know who the hell this person is.
Has a lively nature.	Is a pain in the neck and will never sit down and shut up.
Has an enquiring mind.	Asks me questions that I can't answer.
Always tries his/her hardest.	But never manages to achieve anything.
Very helpful.	The only person who doesn't tell me to get knotted when I ask him/her to clear up the art work mess or fetch me a cup of coffee.

School

Has settled in quickly.	I'm still not sure who this person is.
Has a forceful personality.	Swears, bullies other kids and I wish he/she was in someone else's group.
Works sensibly and quietly.	No, sorry. I still can't think who this nonentity is.
Is a valued member of the group.	I can just about put up with them.
Has a humorous nature.	Tells jokes all the time instead of working.
Will go far.	Preferably Tibet, the Sahara Desert or anywhere away from me.
Has a sensitive nature.	Is a total wimpo.
Progressing well.	Who IS this person?!
Has made a great improvement.	Because he/she couldn't have got any worse.
Could try harder.	He/she is asleep all the time.

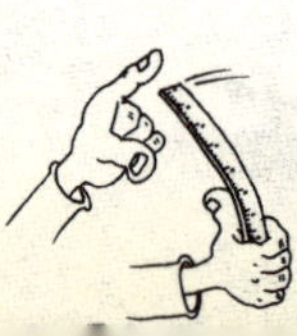

Always gives of his/her best.	But is a total thicko so isn't ever going to get any better.
Is good at language.	Bad language, which is usually directed at me.
Always volunteers.	But is never picked because he/she is useless at everything.
Takes an interest in Chemistry.	Is learning to make explosives.
Has written some interesting pieces.	But I can't understand them.
Seems to be enjoying the subject.	It's no good. I admit it. I do NOT know who this child is. Are you sure he/she exists, or has the computer made a mistake with the class list?
Is good at practical work.	Can't read or write.
Enjoys computing.	Plays computer games all the time.
Takes an interest in Media Studies.	Wants to watch TV instead of working.

THE ABSOLUTELY BRILL AND COMPLETELY REALISTIC UNISEX PHOTOCOPIABLE SCHOOL REPORT

Yes, that's right! For the price of this book, you get not only all the brilliant information that the authors have painstakingly gathered for it, but also this ABSOLUTELY FREE School Report. All you have to do is photocopy it, write your name, form and school in the space provided and show it to your Parent/Guardian/Social Worker/Probation Officer.

BUT THERE'S MORE! On the very next page to your ABSOLUTELY BRILL UNISEX PHOTOCOPIABLE SCHOOL REPORT, you will find an ABSOLUTELY NAFF UNISEX PHOTOCOPIABLE SCHOOL REPORT. All you do with this is photocopy it, fill in the details of your WORST ENEMY and send it to his or her parents. This will certainly lead to your enemy being grounded for the rest of eternity/taken for Educational Counselling/shot at dawn/locked in the attic/buried under a new bridge support on the M25.

NOTES: Please note the following:
1. The Einstein mentioned in the comments on Science is Sid Einstein, who owns Einstein's Wholesale Knitwear.

2. Sorry we can't give you a better report for P.E. The problem is that, in our experience, all P.E. teachers put "Satisfactory Progress" on everyone's school report.

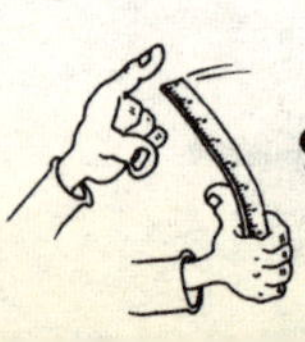

THE NOTIONAL CURRICULUM COUNCIL

REPORT FORM

NOTICE TO SCHOOLS AND PARENTS: THE NOTIONAL CURRICULUM COUNCIL HAS ORDERED THAT THIS REPORT FORM WILL BE USED FOR ALL SCHOOL REPORTS IN NOTIONAL CURRICULUM SUBJECTS. IT REPLACES ALL OTHER REPORT FORMS.

NAME ____________ SCHOOL ________ FORM ________

SUBJECT	COMMENTS	GRADE
ENGLISH	Your essay on "what I did in the holidays" was certainly absolutely brilliant, and I'm sure it will make a superb Mini-Series. Congratulations on your Pulitzer Prize.	A+
HISTORY	Your proof that, in the legend of The Wooden Horse, "Troy" was actually a misprint for "Torquay" led to the discovery of the Horse itself buried under Sainsbury's; probably the greatest historical discovery since the Tomb of Tutankhamen.	A++
GEOGRAPHY	Not everyone would have the courage to prove their theory that the early inhabitants of Greenland came from the Basingstoke area by sailing the Atlantic on a raft made entirely of old bus tickets. Well done!	AA++
LANGUAGES	Speaks all known languages without a trace of accent. Recent translation of "War and Peace" into Inuit a major feat of modern linguistics.	AA+++
MATHS	Makes the Scientific Calculator obsolete.	$Ax10^{23}$
SCIENCE	The greatest scientific brain since Einstein.	$A=MC^2$
PERFORMING ARTS	Your Third Symphony was a triumph at the Last Night of the Proms. I look forward to your forthcoming season at the National Theatre.	AAAAAAA AAAAAAA AAAAAAA
P.E.	Satisfactory Progress.	C+

TUTOR'S COMMENTS It is not often that a school produces a student whose brilliance in all subject areas is beyond calculation, and who is also kind to animals, but you are such a student. It is a pleasure, a privilege and a great honour to have taught you. Your PhD is thoroughly deserved and I look forward to your early canonization.

E. Lush (Ms)

School

THE NOTIONAL CURRICULUM COUNCIL
REPORT FORM

NOTICE TO SCHOOLS AND PARENTS: THE NOTIONAL CURRICULUM COUNCIL HAS ORDERED THAT THIS REPORT FORM WILL BE USED FOR ALL SCHOOL REPORTS IN NOTIONAL CURRICULUM SUBJECTS. IT REPLACES ALL OTHER REPORT FORMS.

NAME ________	SCHOOL ________	FORM ________
SUBJECT	COMMENTS	GRADE
ENGLISH	Has approximately the same command of English as a terminally deranged Yak. Can barely spell the indefinite article. Writing looks like the results of an explosion in a can of Alphabeti Spaghetti.	E-
HISTORY	Cannot remember what happened five minutes ago. Thinks Napoleon Bonaparte was The Man From Uncle. Answer to the question "Why did the Ancient Egyptians build pyramids?" was "To keep the fairies in." Hopeless.	F--
GEOGRAPHY	Gets lost going to the lavatory. Thinks a continental plate is something French people eat off. Frankly, it's my opinion that you couldn't find your bottom with both hands.	U
LANGUAGES	Speaks French like a native – of Estonia. Thinks coup de grace is a lawnmower, and coq au vin is a chicken on a lorry. Totally useless.	U-
MATHS	Cannot count to twenty without taking shoes and socks off.	U-U
SCIENCE	Is working towards understanding the principle that water is wet.	X
PERFORMING ARTS	Forgets which end of a recorder you blow down. Has personality, charisma and talent of a piece of string.	Z-
P.E.	Satisfactory Progress.	C+

TUTOR'S COMMENTS It is regrettable that the laws of this country do not permit students like this to be drowned at birth. I feel it is a judgement on me that I am having to teach this child, who does not have the brains God gave an electric toaster. Repulsive in appearance, stupid beyond belief and prey to disgusting personal habits, this pupil is fit only to be a contestant on "Blind Date".

E. Lush (Ms)

LAST THOUGHTS

Hands up everybody who's ever been told, "If you don't do well at school and pass your exams, you won't get a good job." I believe that's unanimous. Well, don't despair!

ALBERT EINSTEIN is now regarded as one of the greatest thinkers who has ever lived. His work on the Theory of Relativity made him famous. He was awarded the Nobel Prize for Physics in 1912. His formula $E=mc^2$ led to the creation of the atomic bomb (something that he hated) and to most of our current thinking on how the universe works. But, at school, young Albert was regarded as a total blockhead. One of his masters said to him, "Einstein, you will never amount to anything!"

Very Old Joke

A boy's parent said to the teacher: "Just teach him to count to ten. He wants to be a boxing referee!"

Joking apart, what is education for? Obviously, it's to prepare you for life. But what does this mean? Some politicians would say that you only need to learn the skills you're going to use. So, hands up everybody who's ever said, "I don't need to learn French / Algebra / Shakespeare / Quantum Theory... I'm never going to need it."

Thought so.

But think about this. Before the end of apartheid in South Africa, the white government introduced the Bantu Education Act, which tried to limit what black children could learn. The idea was to produce school leavers with just enough knowledge to be servants and factory workers, but not enough to be able to think about issues such as racial prejudice. The result was that black children in almost every school in South Africa went on strike. They held protest marches. Some were killed. Our point is this: those children would rather not learn anything than learn only what the white government thought they "needed to know".

Schools have never been perfect and they're not perfect now, but our final message is:

Don't be put off when people tell you it's a waste of time.

Don't listen to anyone who tells you you can't succeed.

Try to enjoy it if possible.

AND the Best of Luck!

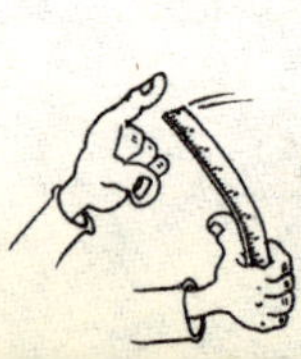

INDEX